THE ART OF WRITING

THE ART OF WRITING

Teachings of the Chinese Masters

Translated and edited by

TONY BARNSTONE

and CHOU PING

SHAMBHALA
Boston & London
1996

Shambhala Publications, Inc.
Horticultural Hall
300 Massachusetts Avenue
Boston, Massachusetts 02115

9 8 7 6 5 4 3 2 1

First Edition

♾ This edition is printed on acid-free paper that meets
the American National Standards Institute Z39.48 Standard.
Distributed in the United States by Random House, Inc.,
and in Canada by Random House of Canada Ltd

Library of Congress Cataloging-in-Publication Data

The art of writing: teachings from the Chinese masters
/ translated and edited by Tony Barnstone and Chou Ping.
—1st ed.   p.   cm.   ISBN 1-57062-092-X (alk. paper)
   1. Chinese literature—History and criticism—Theory, etc.
   2. Chinese poetry—History and criticism—Theory, etc.
I. Barnstone, Tony. II. Chou, Ping. III. Lu, Chi, 261–303.
Wen fu. English. 1996. IV. Ssu-k'ung, T'u, 837–908.
tShih p' in. English. 1996. V. Wei, Ch'ing-chih, fl. 1240–1244.
Shih jen yü hsieh. English. 1996.
        PL2261.A77   1996   95-39570
        895.1'09—dc20   CIP

Cover art: *Purification at the Orchid Pavilion* (detail), handscroll, ink and
color on silk, 1671, 28.1 × 392.8 cm. Fan Yi, Chinese, active ca. 1658–71, Qing
dynasty. © The Cleveland Museum of Art, 1995, Gift of the Junior Council of
The Cleveland Museum of Art and of Mrs. Wai-kam Ho in the name
of the Junior Council, 77.47.

 **PRINTED IN CANADA**

Contents

Acknowledgments

Some of these works have appeared, sometimes in earlier versions, in *The American Poetry Review, Shambhala Sun, The Literary Review,* and Willis Barnstone and Tony Barnstone, eds., *Literature of Asia, Africa and Latin America* (Englewood Cliffs, N.J.: Prentice-Hall, 1996).

Preface
THE MANY FACES OF WRITING

IN contrast to the normally austere and humorless Western tradition of the *ars poetica,* Chinese writers, though sometimes equally pedantic, have through many dynasties made their pronouncements on literature witty and aphoristic, magical and profound, spiritual or satiric. The "Great Preface" to the *Confucian Odes,* the most ancient anthology of Chinese poetry and wellspring of Chinese poetics and poetic thought, assigns poetry great power and the Confucian task of rectifying political and social behavior. Poetry "rights what's wrong, moving heaven and earth, spirits and gods." The Taoists also ascribe great powers to poetry, but their way is more internal, mystical, paradoxical, and humorous. The basic texts of Taoism, the *Tao Te Ching* and the *Chuang-tzu,** which were set down around the second century BCE, convey a celebration of whimsy, spontaneity,

---

*To avoid confusion, we have romanized certain key terms and names (Tao, Ch'i, *Tao Te Ching,* and *Chuang-tzu*) according to the Wade-Giles system, in which they are best known in English. All other Chinese terms are transliterated in the now-dominant pinyin system.

and contradiction, and a metaphysic that often disdains Confucian duty and politics.

In the vein of this ancient tradition are the two Taoist poets whose work opens this book, Lu Ji (261–303 CE) and Sikong Tu (837–908 CE). These poems so beautifully teach and exemplify the craft of writing poetry that they have come to be seen as the masterworks of their creators. While Lu Ji's aesthetic is deeply Taoist, it incorporates strong Confucian elements as well. Lu echoes the concerns of the Great Preface, stating that poetry "can save teetering governments and weak armies; / it gives voice to the dying wind of human virtue." He is also deeply engaged with a Confucian respect for the past—"my heart respects conventional rules / and laws of composition")—but he recognizes the need each day to make the poem new.

The poems of Lu and Sikong take us on extraordinary journeys into the labyrinth of the self and the imagination, and in the process connect us to the hidden source that lies beneath the world. The poet taps this Taoist source in nature for inspiration. From what is beyond words, the poet derives speech. As Lu Ji writes, the poet "knocks on silence to make a sound." With eyes closed to the sensory world, the poet finds a sky and earth inside.

In Sikong Tu's series of twenty-four poems on poetry, the elements that the poet manipulates are at the same time literary and mystical. "Someone hidden controls the world," writes Sikong, and in the world of the poem, the poet is the hidden creator. Like Lu Ji questing for vision through internal space, Sikong Tu takes us on a spirit voyage, whose propelling force is Ch'i. Ch'i is a nebulous Taoist term that refers to an indomitable universal energy that, like the Western concept of the soul or spirit (Latin *animus,* Greek *pneuma*), is also the animating breath. In these poems we are led, perhaps breathed, along a literary path that is also a spiritual road. The art of writing, like the Tao, is by nature indefinable. And like the Tao—the creative force that governs and inhabits the world—it is always changing, and its many faces can never be wholly known. But the attempt to know the Tao is itself a way. In this, the Tao is like Ithaka in Constantine Cavafy's poem of that name. "Do not hurry the journey," Cavafy advises; "Pray that the way be long, full of adventures, full of knowledge." Arrival is not the end. If you find Ithaka poor, she hasn't cheated you, for in your wisdom you will have learned what Ithaka means:

> Ithaka gave you the beautiful voyage.
> Without her you wouldn't have taken the way.

With all its many ports, wild gods, monsters, and sensual and visionary cities, the journey itself reveals Ithaka's multiple aspects. So these Taoist poets offer no absolute solutions, no rewarding and final ends. Rather, they are practical and spiritual instructors in the many contradictory faces of writing, the unity in paradox of which the way is made.

Chinese writers have also given us more than a thousand years of humorous, sardonic prose commentaries and profound parables about the art of writing. The brief texts presented here, many no longer than a few sentences, strive for the evocative compactness of the classical Chinese poem.

They are almost unknown in the West, but their insights into fiction and poetry are so clean and essential that, despite continental distance and the passage of centuries, they make an immensely practical and fun manual for creative writers today. Taoist contradictions are ever-present. Like Ernest Hemingway bluntly telling writers to kill their darlings—to destroy so that they can create—a piece in Song Zijing's collection reads: "Whenever I see my own work I want to burn the poems I hate. Mei Yaochen congratulates me. 'You have made progress.' " These miniature masterpieces are sometimes hilarious. As Oscar Wilde lampoons the impressionist painters of his day in "On the Art of Lying," the Tang poet Li Shangyin (813–858) satirizes the landscape painters and poets of his day in "Ways to Kill a Landscape." He enumerates some of the ways: wash your feet in a clear spring, dry your loincloth upon the flowers, burn your zither to cook a crane, scream underneath a pine tree.

The imperial system of civil service examinations in China, which endured until the early twentieth century, required scholar officials to be versed in the classics and to be practitioners of calligraphy (*shu*) and poetry (*shi*). The cultivated gentlemen of the literati class were supposed to be familiar with several arts: not only poetry and calligraphy, but also zither playing (*qing*), the game of Go (*weiqi*), and painting (*hua*); and these arts, and others as well, came to be intimately related. As Lu Juren observes in his piece on artistic enlightenment, "Inspiration enters at the border between hard work and laziness," and thus when a calligrapher relaxes by watching a woman perform a sword dance, he is suddenly enlightened about the nature of his own art. Though most of the passages presented here deal with poetry, creative writers in all genres will enjoy watching this dance of words. In fact, many of these commentaries edge into short fiction or history as they recount the banquets, conquests, and roadside encounters that took place in China's lost dynasties.

"What's the difference between poetry and prose?" Wang Jiling asks. Wu Qiao answers that a writer's message is like rice:

> When you write in prose, you cook the rice. When you write poetry, you turn rice into rice wine. Cooking rice doesn't change its shape, but making it into rice wine changes both its quality and shape. Cooked rice makes one full, so one can live out one's life span. . . . Wine, on the other hand, makes one drunk— makes the sad happy and the happy sad. Its effect is sublimely beyond explanation.

In this humble culinary comparison, we are confronted once again with the ineffability of artistic creation. As Lu Ji concludes in his own preface, "The spontaneous skills needed to carve a new creation are often beyond words. What can be said, however, is verbalized in what follows."

In the following pages, China offers us a manual of enlightenment in the elusive art of writing.

THE ART OF WRITING

WRITING

Lu Ji

Introduction

THE SPIRIT JOURNEY
OF THE IMAGINATION

L U JI (261–303) was born at the end of the Three
Kingdoms period in the state of Wu, at his family's
estate at Huading in the Yangtze Delta. He came from a
family with a long and distinguished military tradition.
His grandfather, Lu Sun, was a famous general who won
the throne for the first emperor of Wu, for which he was
rewarded with the title of duke and the estate at Huading.
Lu's father and two older brothers all had commands on the
northern frontier, but the weak Emperor Hao ignored his
father's warnings of dangers from the neighboring state of
Jin and lost his empire in a decisive river battle. Both of
Lu's older brothers were killed in this battle. He and his
younger brother escaped to Huading, where they remained
in virtual house arrest for ten years, devoting themselves to
scholarship, poetry, and the study of Confucian and Taoist
thought. At the age of twenty-nine Lu went with his
brother to the Jin court, and the two succeeded in launch-
ing themselves once again into official and military careers.
In his forty-second year, serving as a general for Prince Yin
in a war against the prince's brother, Prince Yi, Lu was

betrayed by another general, who refused to support him in a key battle. Lu's troops were decisively routed, and the river was choked with their bodies. His enemies denounced him to Prince Yin, who caused him to be executed on trumped-up charges of treason. His two sons were also executed. It is said that the night before his death, Lu Ji dreamed he was confined in a carriage draped with black curtains, which he could not break out of. His last words were said to be, "Will I never hear the call of the cranes at Huading again?"

Lu was a prolific writer, but his only major work was a rhyme-prose piece of literary criticism titled *The Art of Writing* (*Wen Fu*). The influence on Chinese literary thought of this relatively short piece cannot be overestimated. *The Art of Writing* sets out to "comment on elegant classics and talk about how strong and weak points find their way into our writings," but it does much more than that. It is valued equally for its critical thought and for its worth as a piece of literature. Its evocation of the writer's preparation to write, of the process through which new poems are catalyzed by the reading of the classics, culminates in a spirit journey of the imagination in which the poet has great Taoist powers to quest through internal and external space and through the literary past. But *The Art of Writing* is both a cosmic treatise and an immensely practical one. From the internal journey of the imagination comes writing in all its styles and genres, many of which Lu Ji catalogues. His *ars poetica*'s sophisticated treatment of the process of writing is its own best exemplar, embodying the virtues that it champions in writing. In addition to questions of style and genre, he addresses revision and the use of key words to "whip the piece like a horse and make it gallop." "To learn writing from classics is like carving an axe handle with an axe—the model is right in your hand," he observes in the preface. Yet the relationship of the writer to works of the past is complex, since what may inspire your work will also kill what you write if you fail to "make it new." He gives writing tips and discusses tone, high and low registers, poetic form, the "dead river" of writer's block, and the "thought wind" of inspiration. His spiritual view of the writing process is mirrored by his faith in the universal power of literature: "With heaven and earth contained in your head, / nothing escapes the pen in your hand."

The Art of Writing is written in a form characterized by rhymed verse interspersed with prose passages and by a pairing of lines in rhetorical parallelism, rather like Western poetry's use of chiasmus. Lu's verse essay is commonly compared with Alexander Pope's *Essay on Poetry* (and with Pope's model, the *Ars Poetica* of Horace) as a great example of literary criticism in verse. The comparison takes on particular relevance when one compares the balanced rhetoric of Pope's rhymed heroic couplets with Lu's parallelism. With characteristic humility, Lu doubts his own ability to get at the essence of writing ("this art can't be captured by the finest words"), but this ineffability itself expresses the spiritual nature of writing. Writing can't express what writing is because it is more than itself; it is an essential relation, a spiritual voyage that connects impulse to action, words to music, and the self to the world.

Translating this notoriously ambiguous text poses special

problems. Many passages are riddles that have countless contradictory solutions, and a tortured and embattled critical commentary has built up around them. It would be possible to burden the text with many footnotes, and many translators do choose to produce ten lines of commentary for each line of poetry. Such valuable scholarship does, however, distract from the poem, as each word or phrase becomes a trapdoor that drops you into a hypertext of criticism and linguistic exegesis. Our interest has been to chart a middle path through a field of warring commentaries and, by making difficult choices between alternate readings, to produce a text that reads fluidly, fluently, and most important, as a poem in English.

Lu Ji's *The Art of Writing* is ancient and contemporary, a masterpiece of world literature. Generations of American poets have been inspired by it. From Lu Ji's work, Gary Snyder learns (in his well-known poem "Axe Handles") the "craft of culture, / How we go on." Poetic craftsmanship is passed from antiquity through the vessel of the word, giving each generation the power to craft their culture anew, and Howard Nemerov (in his poem "To Lu Chi") also receives the word about words from Lu Ji and marvels at how Lu's quiet, clear voice sings, despite centuries of "dust and time," about the delights and difficulties of writing well.

The Art of Writing

PREFACE

AFTER READING many talented writers, I have gained insights into the writing craft. The ways that words and expressions ignite meaning, varied as they are, can be analyzed and critiqued for their beauty and style. Through my own efforts, I know how hard it is to write, since I always worry that my ideas fail to express their subject and that my words are even further removed from insufficient ideas. The problem is easy to understand; the solution is more difficult. So I started writing this rhymed essay to comment on elegant classics and talk about how strong and weak points find their way into our writings. Someday, I hope, it will be thought that I have captured these subtle secrets in words. To learn writing from classics is like carving an axe handle with an axe—the model is right in your hand, but the spontaneous skills needed to carve a new creation are often beyond words. What can be said, however, is verbalized in what follows.

1 The Impulse

A poet stands between heaven and earth
and watches the dark mystery.
To nourish myself I read the classics.

I sigh as the four seasons spin by
and the swarm of living things kindles many
    thoughts.
In rough autumn it hurts to see leaves stripped
    away,
but how tender the soft sprigs in budding
    spring.
Morning frost is awe in my heart,
my ambition floats with high clouds,
I devote songs to ancestors
and sing the clean fragrance of their virtue.
I roam the classics, a forest of treasures,
and love their elegant balance of style and
    substance.
Inspired, I lay down the book I was reading
and let words pour out from my brush.

2 Meditation

At first I close my eyes. I hear nothing.
In interior space I search everywhere.
My spirit gallops to the earth's eight borders
and wings to the top of the sky.
Soon, misty and brightening like the sun about
    to dawn,
ideas coalesce and images ignite images.
When I drink the wine of words
and chew flowers from the Six Books,[1]

---

1. The Confucian classics.

I swim freely in the celestial river
and dive into the sea's abyss.
Sometimes words come hard—they resist me
till I pluck them from deep water like hooked
    fish;
sometimes they are birds soaring out of a cloud
that fall right into place, shot with arrows,
and I harvest lines neglected for a hundred
    generations,
rhymes unheard for a thousand years.
I won't touch a flower already in morning bloom
but quicken the unopened evening buds.
In a blink I see today and the past,
put out my hand and touch all the seas.

3 Process

Search for the words and sphere of thought,
then seek the proper order;
release their shining forms
and tap images to hear how they sing.
Now leaves grow along a branching thought.
Now trace a current to its source.
Bring the hidden into light
or form the complex from simplicity.
Animals shake at the tiger's changing pattern
and birds ripple off when a dragon is seen;
some words belong together
and others don't join, like jagged teeth,

but when you're clear and calm
your spirit finds true words.
With heaven and earth contained in your head,
nothing escapes the pen in your hand.
It's hard to get started at first,
painful like talking with cracked lips,
but words will flow with ink in the end.
Essence holds content as the trunk lifts the tree;
language is patterned into branches, leaves, and
    fruit.
Now words and content match
like your mood and face—
smile when you're happy
or sigh when your heart hurts.
Sometimes you can improvise easily.
Sometimes you only bite the brush and think.

4 The Joy of Words

Writing is joy—
so saints and scholars all pursue it.
A writer makes new life in the void,
knocks on silence to make a sound,
binds space and time on a sheet of silk
and pours out a river from an inch-sized heart.
As words give birth to words
and thoughts arouse deeper thoughts,
they smell like flowers giving off scent,
spread like green leaves in spring;

a long wind comes, whirls into a tornado of
    ideas,
and clouds rise from the writing-brush forest.

5 The Many Styles

But styles are diverse;
there is no absolute standard for anything,
and since things keep changing all the time
how to nail down the perfect description?
Control of language shows an author's skills;
craftsmanship comes when rhetoric pays
    concept's bill.
Writing is a struggle between presence and
    absence.
Wade through the shallows, and if it's deep,
    swim.
It is all right to abandon compass and square
if you are a mirror held up to real shapes.
To seduce the eye use a florid style,
but to please the mind be precise.
Still, a full description can't be confined.
Discourse blooms when it goes beyond words.

6 Genres

Poetry (*shi*) is a bright web of sensuous emotion;
The rhymed essay (*fu*) is clear and coherent as
    an exposition;

stele inscriptions (*bei*) are refined and faithful to
   detail;
an elegy (*lei*) is a painful tangle of sorrow;
inscriptions (*ming*) are gentle and succinct but
   deep in meaning;
didactic compositions (*zhen*) jolt you through
   powerful logic;
odes (*song*) are gentle in tone and graceful in
   style;
explanatory essays (*lun*) are accurate and
   convincing;
memorandums to the king (*zou*) should be proper
   and clear;
written debates (*shuo*) should dazzle with
   eloquence.
Though there are many different genres,
they all oppose deviance and license
and insist you present your argument
with not one wasted word.

7 The Music of Words

Like shifting forms in the world,
literature takes on many shapes and styles
as the poet crafts ideas
into elegant language.
Let different cadences be used in turn
like five colors in harmony,[2]

---

2. Perhaps an early gesture toward metrical regulation based on
the four tones of classical Chinese. The traditional primary colors in
China included white, black, red, yellow, and blue/green.

and though they vanish and reappear
    inconstantly
and though it seems a hard path to climb,
if you know the basic laws of order and change
your thoughts like a river will flow in channels.
But if your words misfire
it's like grabbing the tail to lead the head:
clear writing turns to mud,
like painting yellow on a base of black.

8 Revision

A sentence may contradict what comes before
or trespass on what follows.
Sometimes the idea is good but words fail,
and fine words may make no sense.
In such cases it is wise to set the two apart
since they harm each other when put together.
It is delicate to judge which idea or word works
    better—
a difference finer than a wheat ear's hairs.
Weigh each word on a scale;
use a measuring cord to make your cuts.

9 The Riding Crop

Sometimes your writing is a lush web of fine
    thoughts
that undercut each other and muffle the theme.

When you reach the pole there's nowhere else
 to go—
more becomes less if you try to improve what's
 done.
A powerful phrase at the crucial point
will whip the piece like a horse and make it
 gallop;
though all the other words are in place,
they wait for the crop to run a good race.
A whip is always more help than harm;
stop revising when you've got it right.

10 Making It New

Perhaps thoughts and words blend
into a lucid beauty, a lush growth;
they flame like a bright brocade,
poignant as a string orchestra.
But if you fail to make it new
you can only repeat the past.
Even when your own heart is your loom,
someone may have woven that textile before,
and to be honorable and keep integrity
you must disown it despite your love.

11 Ordinary and Sublime

Flowering forth, a tall rice ear
stands proudly above the mass,
a shape eluding its shadow,

its sound refusing echoes.
The best line is a towering crag.
It won't be woven into an ordinary song.
The mind can't find a match for it
but casts about, unwilling to give up.
After all, jade veins make a mountain shimmer,
pearls in water make the river seductive,
a green kingfisher gives life
even to ragged thornbushes,
and classic and folk songs
blend in a fine contrast.

12 A One-String Harp

When an author composes too short a poem,
it trails off with a lonely feeling
like looking down at solitude with no friends
or peering into the vast sky, disconnected.
One string on a harp is crisp and sweet
but sings without resonance and harmony.

13 Harmony

Trust your words to jangling sounds
and their beauty will lose its luster.
When the ugly and beautiful mix in one body,
the good quality will be stained.
When pipes play too fast for the dancers,
they chase each other without harmony.

14 Heart

When natural reason is sacrificed for
    strangeness—
an absurd and empty quest for trifles—
words are numb and loveless
like drifting souls who can never go home.
It's like plucking a thin string near the bridge:
you make harmonies without heart.

15 Dignity

When you race madly after a choral medley,
seduced by cheap and gaudy sounds,
your flashy poem caters to the vulgar taste
like the rowdy notes of a common tune.
The erotic songs of Fanglu and Shangjian
have a base appeal but have no grace.

16 Overrestraint

But if your poem is too pure and graceful
and free from wild excess,
it's blander than the aftertaste of a spiceless
    broth,
thinner than ghostly harmonics from a temple
    lute.
One singer plus a three-person chorus
is elegant but without allure.

17 Forming Form

Tailor the poem to be plump or slender,
look it over and consider the form.
Make changes when they're apt,
sensitive to the subtle difference they make.
Sometimes raw language conveys clever ideas
and light words carry weighty truth.
Sometimes you wear old clothes yet make them
      new
or discover clarity in the murk.
Sometimes you see it all in a flash,
sometimes it takes a lot of work.
Be like a dancer arcing her long sleeves to music
or a singer improvising to the strings;
like the craft of master wheelwright Bian,[3]
this art can't be captured by the finest words.

18 The Well-Wrought Urn

My heart respects conventional rules
and laws of composition.
I recall the great works of old masters
and see how my contemporaries have failed—

---

3. Chuang-tzu tells of an encounter between wheelwright Bian
and Duke Huan of Chi. Bian told the duke that his craft contained
a subtle, incommunicable essence, which he could not put into
words in order to pass on the trade to his son. Words are shadows of
life, half-expressions. Therefore, Bian concluded, the "words of the
sage" that the duke had been reading were "nothing but dregs."

poems from the depth of a wise heart
may be laughed at by those who are blind.
Poems fine as jade filigree and coral
are common as beans on the plain,
endless like air in the world's great bellows,
eternal as the universe;
they grow everywhere,
but my small hands hold only a few.
My water jar is often empty. It worries me.
I make myself sick trying to expand my pieces.
I limp along with short poems
and patch up my songs with common notes.
I'm never happy with what I've done,
so how can my heart be satisfied?
Tap my work: I fear it clunks like a dusty
     earthen bowl
and I'm shamed by the song of musical jade.

19 Inspiration

As to the flash of inspiration
and traffic laws on writing's path—
what comes can't be stopped,
what leaves will not be restrained.
It hides like fire in a coal
then flares into a shout.
When instinct is swift as a horse
no tangle of thoughts will hold it back:
a thought wind rises in your chest,

a river of words pours out from your mouth,
and so many burgeoning leaves sprout
on the silk from your brush
that colors brim out of your eyes
and music echoes in your ears.

20 Writer's Block

But when the six emotions[4] are stagnant,
the will travels yet spirit stays put—
a petrified and withered tree,
hollow and dry as a dead river.
Then you must excavate your own soul,
search yourself till your spirit is refreshed.
But the mind gets darker and darker
and you must pull ideas like silk from a cocoon.
Sometimes you labor hard and build regrets—
then dash off a flawless gem.
Though this thing comes out of me,
I can't master it with strength.
I often stroke my empty chest and sigh:
what blocks and what opens this road?

21 The Power of a Poem

The function of literature is
to express the nature of nature.
It can't be barred as it travels space

---

4. Sorrow, joy, hate, love, pleasure, anger. The list is changeable, and at times a seventh emotion, desire, is added.

and boats across a hundred million years.
Gazing to the fore, it forms models for people
    to come,
and looking aft, meditates on symbols of the
    ancients.
It can save teetering governments and weak
    armies;
it gives voice to the dying wind of human virtue.
No matter how far, this road will take you there;
it will express the subtlest point.
It waters the heart like clouds and rain,
and shifts form like a changeable spirit.
Inscribed on metal and stone it spreads virtue.
Flowing with pipes and strings, each day the
    word is new.

THE TWENTY-FOUR STYLES OF POETRY

Sikong Tu

Introduction
THE TAO OF WRITING

The Twenty-four Styles of Poetry, an influential Tang dynasty *ars poetica* that categorized classical Chinese poetry into twenty-four styles, or genres, and embodied the essence of each style within a poem, was written by Sikong Tu (837–908). Despite its nominal purpose—to bring clarity and definition to poetic practice—this series of poems is notorious for its own difficult obscurity. Much of its ambiguity derives from Sikong's somewhat ill-defined Taoism (blended with Buddhist and Confucian elements), which permeates these poems and converts many lines into gnomic, mystical riddles that tie commentators and translators up into fantastic knots. Yet the coincidence of inspiration and mysticism, as we have seen in Lu Ji's *The Art of Writing*, can be fortuitous. The imagination *is* sublimely indefinite and slippery, and it does resist being chopped up and constrained into little boxes; so a nomenclature that has a spiritual cast to it may in fact express more about the murky sources of poetry than a rigorously precise one.

In fact, a Taoist changeability and lack of differentiation is the point of many of these poems, as in "The Implicit Style":

> It is dust in timeless open space,
> is flowing, foaming sea spume,

> shallow or deep, cohering, dispersing.
> One out of a thousand contains all thousand.

"The Tao," writes Sikong, "isn't confined by shape. / It's round at times or square." The same goes for that inspirational essence that gives a poem its charge. For Sikong the Tao and the inspirational essence of a poem are not differentiated, either. Thus, poets are practitioners of a divine craft who must perfect themselves internally to achieve perfection in what they write:

> If you free your nature
> you'll have this style.

Such perfection, like spiritual perfection, can only be alluded to, never actually defined: "It is beyond words / and these are clumsy metaphors." It is extraordinarily hard to find, yet it will come to you by itself. It must be achieved through *lack of desire* and through *lack of effort* since in both Taoism and Buddhism, desire, effort, and a grasping attachment to the world are precisely what chain us to our mundane state.

Sikong came from Shanxi Province, from a distinguished family of government servants, but he himself had an unglamorous career as a minor official, marked by banishments and political instability. Nevertheless, he was celebrated in his time for both his poems and his criticism. He was powerfully influenced by the Confucian tradition and later, frustrated in his official career, turned to Taoism and Buddhism. It is said that when the Tang dynasty was overthrown and Li Yu, the last Tang emperor, was murdered, Sikong starved himself to death in protest.

THE TWENTY-FOUR STYLES OF POETRY

1 The Masculine and Vital Style

As great calf muscles bulge in use,
the spiritual body swells inside;
with a return to energy of the primal void
comes potency and masculine strength.

Ten thousand things are contained in this style.
It stretches from end to end of space—
a boundless wilderness of clouds flowing like oil
or a long wind coming from infinity.

Beyond all appearances,
you will find it at the circle's center. [1]
Hold it without effort
and it will come to you without end.

---

1. The center of the circle suggests emptiness, uselessness, the invisible Taoist source. As the *Tao Te Ching* says, "Form a vessel out of clay; / the emptiness inside makes it useful. / Cut out doors and windows to make a room; / the holes make it useful. / Thus, you gain from what is present, / but usefulness comes from absence."

2 The Placid Style

Dwell plainly in calm silence,
a delicate heart sensitive to small things.
Drink from the harmony of yin and yang,
wing off with a solitary crane;[2]

and like soft breezes
trembling in your gown,
the rustle of slender bamboo,
a beauty will stay with you.

You meet this style by not trying deeply.
It thins to nothing if you approach,
and even when its shape seems near
it can turn all wrong inside your hand.

3 The Graceful Style

Flowing water gleams and gleams
and far-off spring is lushly blooming.
Deep in a serene valley,
glimpses of a beautiful woman.

Emerald peaches. The trees are full.
A riverbank of wind, sun, and water.
In the willow shade a road zigzags.
Orioles pour with song, one next to the other.

Ride it far and it will take you farther.
The more you gaze, the clearer its truth.

---

2. An allusion to a number of Chinese tales in which Taoists who
become immortal fly off on the back of a crane.

If this style isn't to be exhausted
you must take the old and make it new.

4 The Potent Style

Green woods, a wild hut.
Setting sun in the transparent air.
I take off my headcloth, walk alone,
often hearing the calls of birds.

No flying swan brings me messages
from my friend traveling so far.
Yet the one I miss *isn't* far.
In my heart we are together.

Ocean wind through emerald clouds.
Night islets and the moon, bright.
After one good line, stop.
A great river spreads across your path.[3]

5 The Ancient Heavenly Style

The Taoist master rides the Ch'i,
a lotus flower in his hand,
floating through cycles of time and space
darkly invisible, leaving no trace.

---

3. This last line suggests the dangers of overwriting. If you go on too long, you walk right out of this style. A good line stops you like a great river and echoes profoundly inside you. A similar effect is described in this Tang-dynasty couplet: "The song is over, the musician gone, / but the river and green mountains keep singing."

Moon rises by the eastern polestar
and a good wind follows.
Hua Mountain is blue at night.
A bell's clean sound is heard.

With elemental spirit in your empty heart
you rise above this dusty world
like the ancient Yellow Emperor and wise
    King Yao,[4]
unique with the essence of Tao.

6 The Classic and Elegant Style

I buy wine with a jade pot.
In my straw-roofed hut I like the rain.
Fine scholars sit at my table.
Bamboo stands high to left and right.

White clouds and sun just after rain.
Hidden birds chase each other.
I sleep in green shade with my lute.
Over there, a flying waterfall.

Falling flowers are speechless.
Like a chrysanthemum I desire nothing.
Write about the year's flowering days
and your poems will be read with joy.

---

4. Traditionally the Yellow Emperor and King Yao were held up
as exemplary moral and spiritual leaders.

7 The Washed and Refined Style

Like ore becoming gold
or lead transformed to silver,
I work to smelt the poem
and love the unbreakable and unstainable.[5]

Spring will pour out of a pond if it's transparent.
Ancient mirrors reflect the spirit if polished.
A clean body gathers purity;
I ride the moon to return to the Tao.

I look at the constellations
and sing about the hermits.
In flowing water today—
the bright moon of my previous body.

8 The Vigorous Style

The spirit traveling as if through space
and moving its Ch'i like a rainbow
is like Wu Gorge, three thousand yards of
        rapids,
or running clouds linking in the wind.

Drink Ch'i and eat power,
preserve purity and guard your heart,

---

5. An allusion to a passage from Confucius's *Analects*, which asks,
"Isn't a thing hard if you grind it but it doesn't thin down? Isn't it
white if black dye won't stain it?"

and you'll move with the force of planets.
This is called storing up potency.

This style is like the heavens and earth:
all move to the same laws.
Seek it through facts
and you'll control it to the end.

9 The Decorative and Pretty Style

When your spirit is wealthy
you take gold lightly.
Ink dries when too thick;
a light wash is often deeper.

Leftover mist by the water
where red apricots flower in the forest.
By my ornamented house, the bright moon
and a painted bridge in green shade.

Gold goblets are brimful of wine
as I play the zither to entertain my guests.
I feel so happy, fulfilled.
My heart is exhausted with joy.

10 The Natural Style

Bend over anywhere and pick it up—
but you can't take it from your neighbors.
Go with the Tao
and what you write is fine as spring.

It's like meeting flowers in bloom,
like seeing the year renew.
Once given to you it can't be stolen,
but gain it by force and soon you're poor again.

A hermit in the empty mountain
after rain collects duckweed
and gains this calm inspiration,
moving about unhurried as heaven's potter's
    wheel.

11 The Implicit Style

Without a single word
the essence is conveyed.
Without speaking of misery
a passionate sadness comes through.

It's true, someone hidden controls the world;
with that being you sink or float.
This style's like straining full-bodied wine
or like a flower near bloom retreating into bud.

It is dust in timeless open space,
is flowing, foaming sea spume,
shallow or deep, cohering, dispersing.
One out of a thousand contains all thousand.

12 The Bold and Unconstrained Style

Observe creation without taboos.
Swallow a vast wilderness, then spit it out again.
With the Tao you return to Ch'i
and are everywhere unconstrained.

A sky wind is waves crashing on waves
and sea mountains are blue and bluer:
you're so full inside with true strength
that ten thousand images are at your command.

One gesture summons sun, moon, and stars
or makes the phoenix follow behind.
At dawn you whip six great turtles that carry
    the earth
and wash your feet at the giant tree where sun
    rises.

13 The Vital Spirit Style

Want to return to the endless source?
Expect it and it will come to you
like a stream bed through bright ripples.
A strange flower has just been conceived.

In green spring, a parrot.
Willow twigs, and towers by a pond.
Jade mountain. A hermit comes.
Clear wine in a deep glass.

With this vitality you travel far
with no trace of dead ashes.
It creates the nature of nature.
Who can possibly judge you?

14 The Careful and Meticulous Style

This craft leaves tangible marks,
but they're almost invisible.
With your images poised to leap into life,
your creation is already amazing:

flowing water, a flower opens.
A clear dewdrop about to dry.
Long main roads are distant,
small roads zigzag slowly.

With language not too elaborate,
thoughts not stagnant,
this style is a green spring field
or bright moon on snow-covered ground.

15 The Carefree and Wild Style

Abide by your nature,
honest and unrestrained.
Whatever you pick up makes you rich
when candor is your friend.

Build your hut below a pine,
toss off your hat and read a poem.
You know if it's morning or evening
but have no idea what dynasty it is.

Do what fits your whim.
Why bother to achieve?

If you free your nature
you'll have this style.

16   The Lucid and Rare Style

Through bright and slender pines
shivering ripples flow.
Sunlit snow covers the strand.
Across the water, a fishing boat.

A pleasant person, jadelike,
in clogs, seeks hidden landscapes,
strolling, then pausing,
as the sky's empty blue goes on and on.

This spirit is ancient and rare
but so limpid it can't be held—
like moonlight at dawn,
a hint of autumn in the air.

17   The Oblique and Winding Style

Climbing in the Taihang Mountains,
sheep-gut paths twist through greenery.
Dark clouds flow like jade,
and the smell of flowers lingers.

Act only when the time is right,
like the melody of a Tibetan flute.
When it seems to fade it's returning.
It's hard to find yet isn't hidden.

Water patterns swirl and eddy
as the storm bird gyrates.[6]
The Tao isn't confined by shape.
It's round at times or square.

18 The Actual Scene Style

Use very straight speech,
without design or deep calculation.
Chancing upon a hermit
is seeing the heart of the Tao.

A clear brook zigzags
through shade of emerald pines.
One man carries firewood,
one is listening to a zither.

Go where your temperament leads.
Not seeking makes it splendid.
With luck you'll stumble on
this rare and crystalline sound.[7]

---

6. What we refer to here as the storm bird, called the *peng* in Chinese, is equivalent to the giant roc of *The Thousand and One Nights*. Chuang-tzu says, "There is a bird named Peng whose back is large as Mount Tai, with wings hanging down like clouds. It rides the tornado up into the sky for thirty thousand miles."

7. The sense of this poem is that a writer may chance on marvelous scenes that couldn't be achieved by design, as the Tao is found only through lack of effort. A Qing dynasty commentator, Sun Liankui, finds this style in the following couplet by his friend Yuanhai: "Where the moon doesn't reach / The sound of the spring is darker." The synesthesia of this moment comes directly from nature, not from overthinking.

19 The Sad and Poignant Style

A typhoon rolls up the waters,
forests are smashed.
This sadness feels like death.
You summon Peace. She doesn't come.[8]

A hundred years flow away
and wealth and nobleness are cold ash.
With the Tao fading day by day,
who can be a hero?

A noble warrior wipes his sword.
His sorrow fills the world
as falling leaves sift and shift
and rain dribbles over dark moss.

20 The Descriptive Style

Powerfully focus your spirit
and turn over clear and authentic images
as if seeking reflections in water
or sketching a day in sun-drenched spring.

Shifting shapes of wind and clouds,
the flowering spirit of grass,

---

8. In this complicated line, Sikong uses an ancient symbol to refer to unattainable ideals. The saddened poet summons beauty, peace, and his ideals as one might summon a lover or a deep friend, but the call is unanswered. Commentators say that this line alludes to the great poet Qu Yuan, who addresses his Fair One—that is, his king—from exile in the famous poem "Encountering Sorrow."

the wave-torn sea
and broken mountain crags —

these are like the Tao.
All attuned, they share the same dust.
Capture the semblance yet change the shape
and you almost master this style.

21 The Transcendent Style

It's not the spirit working.
It's not from nature's enigma.
It's the way white clouds
return on a clear wind.

Seen far off it seems apparent,
but it changes when you approach.
With even a Breath of Tao
you'll end up different from the rest.

Jumbled mountains, tall trees,
emerald moss, sunlight —
chant these things, think on them
till all sounds taper off.

22 The Floating and Serene Style

In deep isolation, ready to take off,
one is proud and aloof
like the crane from Hou Mountain[9]
or clouds at the peak of Hua Mountain.

A hermit with harmony inside
has a mild and smiling face.
A flying weed tumbling on the wind,
he floats across boundless space.

Hard to grasp this style,
but you can almost hear it.
Those who understand, wait.
If you desire it, it will retreat.

23 The Big-Hearted and Expansive Style

We live no more than a hundred years,
not too long before we depart.
Happiness is bitterly short;
gloom and fretting abound.

Why not take a jar of wine
and each day visit the misty wisteria?

---

9. This line alludes to a tale from *Biographies of the Immortals* in which the immortal Wang Ziqiao flies off from the top of Hou Mountain on the back of a white crane.

Let flowers cover the straw-thatched roof.
Let mountain showers pass over.

When wine is finished
take a vine stick and sing out loud.
What life doesn't end in death?
Only South Mountain can last.[10]

24 The Flowing Style

It takes in like a water mill
and turns like a pearl marble.
It is beyond words
and these are clumsy metaphors.

Earth spins on a hidden axis
and the universe rolls slowly around its hub.
If you search out the origin
you'll find a corresponding motion.

Climb high into spiritual light.
Then dive deep into dark nothing.
All things for thousands of years
are caught up in the flow.

---

10. South Mountain is famous in Chinese poetry as a place of Taoist peace and quietude. It often appears in the poetry of Wang Wei and Tao Yuanming.

POETS' JADE SPLINTERS

Edited by

Wei Qingzhi

Introduction

A Cluster of Critical Gems

Poets' Jade Splinters is an extraordinary Song dynasty collection of aphoristic prescriptions for writers, humorous anecdotes about poetry and poets, epigrammatic commentaries, and rules for composing literature. It is considered the finest collection of its type, reflecting the excellent taste of its editor, Wei Qingzhi. Wei was a native of Fuzhou City, Fujian Province. Very little is known about him. We don't know when he was born or died, and not much is known of his life except that, despite indications of great talent, he eschewed the path of the scholar official. We also know that he was a great lover of chrysanthemum bushes—so great that he planted a thousand of them!

Wei's twenty-volume anthology brings together a superlative collection of brief jottings in a form called *shi hua,* which translates as "poetry talk," or "comments on poetry." Though Wei's dates are unknown, and we don't know when he completed the collection, we do know that Huang Sheng's preface was written in 1244, so the book must have been compiled before then. It is a compilation of earlier works, some of them dating from the Tang dynasty or earlier, though the genre of "poetry talk" is considered to have originated later, in the Song dynasty, with a much-imitated collection of twenty-eight literary commentaries by Ouyang Xiu (1007–1072) that he titled simply *Comments on Poetry* (it later took the name *Mr. Six-One's Comments on Poetry*). In fact many of Ouyang's comments are included in *Jade Splinters*, though in expanded, contracted, and otherwise adapted forms. With one exception, we've chosen to separate out Ouyang's comments and translate them from more authoritative sources for inclusion in the following section. Ouyang's modest goal in his work was to make a collection that would "aid casual conversation," and while later authors and compilers continued to value casually pithy and humorous comments, they also set more serious goals of distinguishing genres, recording virtue, and systematizing the writing of literature. Taoist, Buddhist, and Confucian elements run throughout the selections included in *Jade Splinters*, and the title itself alludes to a Taoist alchemical medicine said to grant immortality. It may also refer metaphorically to the process of writing poetry as one of cutting gems. These critical jottings are like jade dust and splinters—a beautiful by-product.

The poetic advice given by the many authors of *Jade Splinters* will sound familiar to teachers of creative writing today: all clichés must go; be specific; too much effort can kill the flow; ruthlessly discard whatever doesn't work; simplicity is hard to achieve; you can't be a writer if you're too lazy to read. When wrapped in a tale, a joke, a fascinating metaphor, or an apt example, such poetic medicine goes down very easily. Like the aphorisms of Nietzsche or

Wallace Stevens, the literary humor of Oscar Wilde, or the letters and prose jottings of Rainer Maria Rilke, these brief wonders skewer and explode pomposity, nail down essential truths, and record the literary musings of great minds in concentrated form.

Poets' Jade Splinters

Prescriptions for Poetry

Comments on poetry are like doctors' prescriptions: if they are not accurate they are useless, as a bad prescription has no medical value. Only a good doctor can judge if the prescription is effective or not, and only a good poet can know if the comments are right or not. This compilation is no easy job.

from the preface to POETS' JADE SPLINTERS,
by Huang Sheng

Burning Poetry

Whenever I see my old work, I want to burn the poems I hate. Mei Yaochen congratulates me: "You have made progress."

from SONG ZIJING'S NOTES

Don't Walk behind Others

For your work to pass through the generations, you must have your own distinctive style. If you always use a compass to draw a circle and a ruler to draw a square, you will always remain a slave. As the ancients say, you can't build a house inside a house. Lu Ji says to avoid the morning flower in full blossom and gather instead evening buds that are not yet open. Han Yu says all clichés must go—this is the essence of prose. *The Book of the Hermit Fisherman of Zhao River* points out that this is also true of poetry. If you just repeat clichés and imitate old works without any change or original ideas, how can you become a famous poet? Huang Luzhi writes that if you follow someone you will always be behind. The first taboo in writing is to walk behind others.

from SONG ZIJING'S NOTES

Don't Beat the Ducks!

Lu Shilong, the governor of Xuan State, used to enjoy caning the women registered as courtesans, the "Government Prostitutes" who served the officials. These singing girls often tried to escape, but they couldn't get away from him. Then a Hangzhou courtesan arrived in Xuan State. Because of her beauty and talent, Shilong grew very fond of her and wouldn't allow her to depart. One day a local courtesan committed a minor offense, and when Shilong was about to cane her again, she pleaded in tears, "I don't want to deny my guilt. I'm just afraid that this beating will make the lady from Hangzhou scared." So Shilong pardoned her and let her go. On hearing of this incident, Mei Yaochen wrote the following poem:

Don't beat the ducks!
You will scare the swan.
The swan that lands on the pond's north shore
is not an old bald bird on a lonely islet.
Even the bald bird want to fly off,
so wouldn't a swan with her long wings?

from THE HERMIT'S COMMENTS ON POETRY

Enlightenment

To compose you need enlightenment. But this comes only from hard work; there's no way to stumble upon it.

from LUI'S RULES FOR SCHOOLCHILDREN

Sword and Brush

If you write with enlightenment, your work will naturally be better than your contemporaries'. Inspiration enters at the border between hard work and laziness. In this way Zhang Changshi, watching Madame Gong Sun doing a sword dance, was suddenly enlightened about the art of calligraphy. Zhang's heart had been so focused on his calligraphy that when he saw this dance he gained insight into the heights of his own art. Someone else watching the sword dance would consider it irrelevant. This is true for both calligraphy and for writing.

—Lu Juren

Rustic Poems

Wang Jian wrote,

> I close the gate to keep the wild deer in
> and share my food with pheasants.

Wei Ye wrote some similar lines:

> When I wash my inkstone, fish drink black ink;
> when I boil my tea, cranes escape from the smoke.

These two poets are trying to describe a hermit's life, but they are writing nonsense. How could the deer and the pheasants be so tame? It would never happen. Wei Ye's poem, at least, is remotely possible. Compare a line such as "The birds have become tame, eating food from my stoop" or Su Dongpo's couplet "I always leave rice scraps for the mice; / I pity the moths, so I don't light my candles." These lines are more reasonable, and people won't make fun of them.

from YU YING COMMENTS ON POETRY

Ways to Kill a Landscape

Yi Shan {another name for the Tang poet Li Shangyin} wrote many miscellaneous pieces, then divided them into more than ten categories. One humorous category was called "Ways to Kill a Landscape." Here are some examples:

Wash your feet in a clear spring.
Dry your loincloth upon the flowers.

Build your house against a mountain.
Burn your zither to cook a crane.
Drink tea in front of the flowers.
Scream underneath a pine tree.

—from XIQING COMMENTS ON POETRY

Advice for Beginners

It's better to be clumsy than clever, better plain than affected, better crude than weak, better eccentric than vulgar. This is true for poetry, as for prose.

from COMMENTS ON POETRY, *by Hou Shan*

You Can't Force It

Poetry cannot be forced. It hits you when mood, time, and place converge. It's good by itself. Have a general idea in mind before writing a poem. A long poem should turn at least three times.

—Shan Gu

Be Specific

Good poetry shines brighter than other poems. When different poets write on the same subject, the gems stand out. When I traveled along the road to Sichuan and stopped at Zhoubi Station, I recalled two famous lines by Shi Manqing:

In my mind water flows into the distance.
Outside my sorrow the old mountains are still green.

Although people like these two lines, to me it seems they could describe almost any place, even though they were written about this station.

from THE EYE OF POETRY

Don't Try Too Hard

Huang Luzhi said to Guo Gongpu, "Why do you try so hard when you write poems?" This is to the point—a good lesson for beginners.

—Xu Yanzhou

Convey the Idea, Not the Name

Su Dongpo says, "Good painters paint the spirit, not the form. Good poets convey the idea, not the name." Here is a poem by him:

Comparing a painting to the object
is how a child judges paintings.
If you think your poem is the last word on a subject,
it shows you're not a poet.

from FORBIDDEN MEAT

Self-Portrait

At the end of the Five Dynasties period, Nan Chuchai, from Haolian, traveled to the state of Yin. The governor there wanted to marry him to his daughter. Chuchai already had a wife named Xie, but he decided to accept this mark of the governor's favor and sent someone back home to fetch his lute and his scrolls, showing no intention of returning to his first wife. On hearing this, Xie, who was a talented painter and writer, painted a self-portrait in front of a mirror and wrote this poem:

> Before I use my painter's red and green brush,
> I pick up my jade mirror.
> It's a surprise to see my lonely face
> and I feel my hair withering.
> It's easy to paint these teary eyes
> but hard to paint the pain inside.
> I'm afraid you'll forget all about me,
> so please look at this portrait sometimes.

Chuchai felt very ashamed of himself when he received the painting and the poem, and he gave up the new marriage, went back to Xie, and stayed with her for the rest of his life.

from THE LOST HISTORY OF THE TANG
AND SONG DYNASTIES

One-Word Master

When Zheng Gu was at Yuanzhou, Zai Ji visited him and presented his poems. Here are two lines from his poem "Early Plum Blossoms":

> Deep snow in the next village.
> Several branches blossomed last night.

Zheng Gu commented: if "several branches" have bloomed, they are not "early" blossoms, so it's better to say "one branch." Zai Ji saluted him as a teacher. Since then, Chinese scholars have referred to Zheng Gu as One-Word Master.

from SUPPLEMENTS TO FIVE DYNASTIES, *by Tao Yue*

Lines Should Not Be Redundant

Poets between the Jin dynasty and the Song dynasty wrote many good lines, but they often used two lines to say the same thing. Here are two examples:

> The new lotus trembles as fish play.
> Petals fall when birds scatter.

> Cicada cries quiet the forest.
> Bird calls darken the mountains.

Lines like these are not bad; the problem is redundancy.

from COMMENTS ON POETRY, *by Cai Kuanfu*

Redundancy, Again

Looking at the examples given above, Wang Anshi suggested replacing the line "Bird calls darken the mountains" with "The wind stops but petals still drop"; in this way the first line suggests motion within stillness, and the next line creates stillness within motion.

from SHENG KUO'S NOTES

Good Lines

When Song Lugong saw good lines, he always wrote them on his study wall. For example:

> Nothing can stop the flowers from falling.
> Like old acquaintances, swallows return.
>
> Quietly I search out the woodpecker's hiding place.
> Calmly I watch a silk spider thread float to earth.

from BLACK BOX NOTES

Roll Call of Ghosts and Doctor Mathematics

Wang, Yang, Lu, and Luo are famous for their poetry. But people comment on their poetic diseases. For example, Yang likes to use names of ancient people; we call this the "roll call of ghosts." Luo likes to use numbers in his poetry; people refer to him as "Doctor Mathematics."

from JADE SPRING

The Elliptical Method

When Zheng Gu writes a poem about falling leaves, he doesn't mention them directly, yet people can infer the subject matter from his poem:

> It's hard for returning ants to find their holes,
> easy for birds to see their nests.

The monk is never sick of them covering the porch,
but a layman will find one of them too much.

from THE COLD STUDY

The Disease of Unintentional Similarity

When Cheng Shimeng was the governor of Hongzhou, he
built a meditation room at his residence. He loved this
room so much that he went there every day, and he inscribed these two lines on a stone:

No matter how busy, I come here once a day.
I often come at midnight, carrying a lantern.

Li Yuangui saw this inscription and laughed, saying, "This
is a poem about going to the toilet!"

from EAST WINDOW NOTES

Three Ways to Steal

There are three kinds of plagiarism in poetry writing. The
clumsiest thief steals the words. Cheng Ju's line "The light
of sun and moon is heavenly virtue" is from Fu Changyu's
line "The light of sun and moon is transparent." The second
kind of plagiarist steals the idea. Consider Shen Chenqi's
lines:

The remains of summer flee from a small pond.
Coolness returns to the tips of tall trees first.

Now consider the original lines by Liu Hun:

> Ripples arise in the pool.
> Autumn comes to tall poplar trees.

The third type of theft doesn't leave much trace. Wang Changlin's lines go:

> With two carp in my hand
> I watch wild geese fall into distance.

The original lines by Qi Kang are

> My eyes see off migrating cranes.
> Holding up my zither, I wave.

from VARIETIES IN A POETIC GARDEN

Don't Leave Traces and Don't Get Stuck

You must shape a poem the way you cut a gem, leaving no traces of your tools. Aim for a bull's-eye, but don't get stuck there. This is what makes poetry so hard. Consider these two lines about willow trees by Li Shangyin:

> Before leaves bud, spring starts to move.
> Countless weeping willow branches shake the dawn.

The marks of the poet's tools are too obvious here. Here is another example, Shi Manqing's poem about plum blossoms:

> You might take it for a peach tree, but it has no
> green leaves.

> You might take it for an apricot tree, but it has
> mossy branches.

This one is so restricted to its subject that it gets stuck.

— Anonymous

Clichés Must Go

A friend came to me with a poem that began, "Coldness in November . . . ," so I asked him, "Have you noticed how Du Fu uses the names of the months in his poems? For example, 'The waves swell in March.' Here, March is used because it is early for large waves to be seen. Another example is 'June comes with cold wind and cold sun.' June is used because such late coldness is unusual. But many of us write lines like 'Coldness in November' when we should avoid such obvious expressions."

from THE EYE OF POETRY

Dexterity in a Single Word

In each line there should be a key word that will act like a magic pill or a Midas touch to make the line work. For example, Meng Haoran writes,

> Thin clouds dilute the sky's silver river.[1]
> Scattered raindrops tap on leaves of the parasol tree.

---

1. The Milky Way.

The key words in these two lines are "dilute" and "tap"; without them these lines wouldn't be good. Mr. Chen once purchased a collection of Du Fu's poetry in which many characters were missing.[2] For example, here is a line in which the last character was absent:

The weightless body of a bird _____

Mr. Chen asked his guests to complete the line. People suggested "shoots by" or "lands" or "soars" or "descends," but no one could agree on the best word. Later, Mr. Chen got a better edition of Du Fu's poems and found that the line actually read: "The weightless body of a bird flickers by." Mr. Chen sighed and admitted that Du Fu's original word was much better.

from THE BOOK OF THE HERMIT
FISHERMAN OF ZHAO RIVER

Plain and Natural

First master elegance, and then strive for the plain style. Nowadays many people write clumsy, facile poems and flatter themselves that they've mastered the plain style. I can't help laughing at this. Poets know that simplicity is difficult. There are poems that illustrate the rigor the plain style demands:

---

2. The second part of this commentary also appears in Ouyang Xiu's *Mr. Six-One's Comments on Poetry*.

Today as in ancient times
it's hard to write a simple poem.

—Mei Yaochen[3]

The lotus flower rises from clear water
naturally, without ornament.

—Li Bai

Plain and natural lines are best.

from SUNNY AUTUMN RHYMED LANGUAGE

Some Lines by Xie Lingyun

Spring grass grows in the low pond.
Weeping willows become singing birds.

Many people have trouble understanding why these lines
are good, because they want something outlandish. These
lines work because they are spontaneous, without too much
gem cutting, yet you wouldn't be able to write them with
common sense alone. The heart of the poet's secret is right
here. Those who try too hard don't understand.

from SHI LING'S COMMENTS ON POETRY

---

3. Mei Yaochen, like Tao Yuanming, is considered an exemplary
plain-style poet; but his work, unlike that of Tao Yuanming, comes
in for some criticism. Mei An, for example, writes, "Mei Yaochen's
poetry is not plain, it's dry."

Some Lines by Tao Yuanming

> Gathering chrysanthemum by the east fence
> my lazy eyes meet South Mountain.

Su Dongpo says that those who don't comprehend poetry want to change these lines by Tao Yuanming, turning the word "meet" into "watch." This is trading jade for garbage. Bai Juyi tried to emulate Tao's lines like so:

> Occasionally I pour a cup of wine,
> sitting and watching Southeast Mountain.

I think this is a very poor imitation.[4]

from NOTES FROM FU'S STUDY

Read More and Write More

The secret of writing lies in reading more and writing more. Many writers worry about writing too little, yet they are too lazy to read. Whenever they write a poem they want it to be the best one around, but it's almost impossible for such writers to achieve this. By constantly writing you will learn to diagnose faults and diseases in what you write, and you won't have to wait for others to point them out.

—*Su Dongpo*

---

4. Tao Yuanming's famous lines are cherished for the way they suggest the joining of the poet with nature through the lack of active looking; the poet encounters the mountain naturally as he looks up, as if running into a friend. Bai Juyi, on the other hand, is actively watching his mountain; this suggests a distance from nature.

Epigrammatically Succinct Lines

There was a poet named Guo Xiangzhen who became famous because of a line written by Mei Yaochen about him: "At the quarry in the moonlight I heard the banished immortal again." These lines suggest that Guo is Li Bai's reincarnation ["Banished Immortal" was Li's nickname]. The best-known lines by Guo Xiangzhen are these:

> Endless flight of birds across the blue evening sky.
> Wind in the reeds when the fisherman stops singing.

When Su Dongpo was prefect of Qiantang, Guo Xiangzhen visited him and showed him a scroll of his poems. Then he gave a reading in a voice so loud that it shook up his audience. Afterward he asked Su Dongpo, "What do you think of my poems?" Su Dongpo replied, "One hundred percent good." Flattered and surprised, Guo asked, "Really? In what way?" Su answered, "Seventy percent oration and thirty percent poetry!"

from WANG ZHIFANG'S COMMENTS ON POETRY

Push or Knock

When the monk Jia Dao came to Luoyang, monks were forbidden to leave the monastery after noon. Jia Dao wrote a sad poem about this, and Han Yu liked the poem so much he helped him get permission to become a layman. The story of their famous meeting follows.

When Jia Dao was concentrating on his poems he would often run into important people without being aware of it.

One day, riding his donkey, he was thinking about these lines:

> Birds return to their nests in trees by the pond.
> A monk is knocking at a door by moonlight.

He couldn't decide whether to replace the word "knocking" with "pushing," so he was making wild gestures on his donkey, acting out first a knock and then a push. While doing this he encountered the procession of the mayor, Han Yu, and neglected to give way. Arrested by the bodyguards and brought before Han Yu, he was asked to explain his actions. He explained that he had been trying to decide between the two words. Han Yu considered this for a long time and said at last, " 'Knocking' is better." They became fast friends after that.[5]

from NOTES OF XIANG SU

The Boat over the Moon

A Korean diplomat was traveling in a boat across the sea, and he started to improvise a poem:

> Waterfowl float and dive.
> Mountain clouds part and blend.

The poet Jia Dao, hearing this, pretended to be an oarsman, and completed the poem:

---

5. This is a famous story, so famous that even today when Chinese writers have to decide between alternate words, they ask, " 'Push' or 'knock?' "

> Oars cut through the sky in the waves.
> The boat skates over the moon in the water.

The Korean diplomat exclaimed, "Excellent! Really good!"
And after that he never talked about poetry again.[6]

from NOTES FROM JINSHI HALL

Butterfly Xie

Scholar Xie has written three hundred poems about butter-
flies, so people call him "Butterfly Xie." He has some good
lines. For example:

> Glimpses of butterflies in wild pursuit of willow
> catkins.
> No way to find them when they dance into pear
> flowers.

> Spring evening: river and sky, and a warm, thin
> wind.
> Butterflies trail the flower peddler across the bridge.

In ancient poetry there are lines like:

> Over the path through the field butterflies slant off.
> Among flowers their wings float them backwards.

> Its body is all powdered like a dandy,
> its heart a Don Juan, stealing fragrance.[7]

These lines are not as profound as Xie's.

from OLD AND NEW COMMENTS ON POETRY

---

6. The Korean diplomat was ashamed to be bested poetically by
someone he thought was a common oarsman.

7. The Chinese Don Juan is Han Shou. For clarity's sake we sub-
stitute his Western counterpart here.

Record of a Dream

Li Zhenyan, also known as Xi Gu, once dreamed that he
went to a palace where hundreds of courtesans were tossing
silk balls around.[8] Each of them sang out a poem, but when
he woke up, he could only remember three of the poems:

> The feast goes all day and night.
> The moon is flowing on the jade steps.
> At dawn I feel the most favored
> and ask others to help me find my silk ball.[9]

> A clear autumn is locked in the Sui dynasty palace,
> which once saw Chanjuan tossing the silk ball.[10]
> Now the gold keys and jade flutes are silent.
> Only a tall tower stands against the moon.

> I hate the kings of the Sui dynasty.
> They grab our waists and bed us like mandarin
>   ducks.[11]
> Now I come back to the place where silk balls were
>   tossed,
> and the gold incense burners don't smell sweet as
>   before.

from HOUQING RECORDS

---

8. An ancient courtship game.

9. She feels favored probably because she has slept with an important man.

10. The Sui dynasty is known for its debauchery, and its demise,
like that of the Roman Empire, is commonly attributed to moral
degeneracy. The ruins of the Sui palace commonly appear in Chinese
poetry about morality, sexuality, or the passage of time.

11. Mandarin ducks, which mate for life, are a stock image for
mating, sex, and loyalty.

Poem on Egrets

Zhang Zhong has a poem on egrets that goes:

> From the deepest depths of the dark sea
> the egret catches a perch, then wades back.

Zhang Wenbao comments, "It is good, but the legs of the egret are a little bit too long."

from RECENT EVENTS BY JING LAKE

Three Shadows

Zhang Ziye wrote the following lines:

> Floating duckweed parts and I see the mountain's
> shadow.

> Clouds break open. Moon. The flowers play with
> shadows.

> The swing tosses its shadow over the wall.

As people love these three lines, Zhang has come to be known as "Mr. Three Shadows."

from TALL STUDY COMMENTS ON POETRY

Begging for a Cat

> In autumn, mice go wild because my cat has died.
> They peep into the jars and turn over basins to wake
> me up.

I've heard your cat is expecting a litter of kittens
so I bought these fish strung on a willow branch. May
    I take one home?

This poem is funny and pleasant, and after one thousand
years one still reads the situation as if it's happening right
now.

from COMMENTS ON POETRY, *by Hou Shan*

Great Tang Dynasty Lines

Lines that create a sense of insight:

Treat a horse with respect if you still owe payments.
A borrowed errand boy won't pay you any mind.

— *Yao He*

From this tall tower I'm surprised at the rainstorm's
    vastness.
When the leaves fall the walled city feels empty.

— *Li Dong*

Remote temple. Few monks visit.
Few travelers cross the rickety bridge.

— *Xu Hun*

Lines that carry you into a painting:

The spring tide rushes in as the evening storms.
Nobody on the wild ferryboat — it spins.

— *Wei Yinwu*

Deep in the sun-filled sky—one wild goose.
A slow, solitary sail on the vast sea.

—Li Bai

Near the river village, rain hangs from a cloud.
An overgrown temple edges into the ball of sunset.

—Cen Can

Wind-tossed lotus surprises the bathing birds.
Traveling fish gather in the bridge's shadow.

—Anonymous

Lines about traveling:

The birds have all returned to their trees.
A traveler struggles up a mountain.

—Ren Fan

Stories and Aphorisms about Literature

Introduction

HOW TO CAPTURE
A DRAGON

THE *shi hua* style of commentary on poetics came to be a popular literary form in the Song dynasty. The genre, as exemplified by the writings of Ouyang Xiu, combines biting, incisive comments about poetic craft with a casual tone, a wry wit, and interesting anecdotes. From the time of the Southern Song onward, however, *shi hua* began to shed some of its character of "random jottings," becoming systematic; and arbitrary collections gave way to increasingly orderly compilations. Noted sinologist Stephen Owen observes that this led to a loss of the "original color" and charm of the form and he comments: "the trend toward systematization in some Southern Song *shi hua* should be understood in the context of the popularization of literary studies in the later Southern Song and early Yuan. The Northern Song intellectuals cultivated an appearance of ease; sophisticated discussion of poetry was supposed to be a pastime. In the Southern Song, we find the beginnings of a mass audience, seeking advice on composition from the masters and guidance in judgment. The printing industry of Hangzhou fed the desires of the urban bourgeoisie to participate in elite culture by the transformation of *shi hua* into poetic education."[1]

Often, these comments seem almost to take the form of diary entries, though in fact the best of them are crafted and polished gems. Many of the stories in these collections concern the actions and insights of famous poets, who, one must understand, were the celebrities of their day. These stories were printed for popular consumption and passed around, rather like the bits of gossip and interview snippets that fill today's celebrity magazines (though with a higher purpose). This may be hard to understand today, when poetry is generally removed from the cultural mainstream. It may be hard to imagine that through much of China's history, poetry, along with art, calligraphy, and music, was the grand highway to political and social success.

The commentaries in this section come from widely varying periods and have distinct characteristics. The *Poetry Stories* of Meng Qi are much more consistently narrative in character than the earlier commentaries, and the people discussed are no longer necessarily famous poets. Rather, a poem or a set of poems proves to be the heart of a historical, fictional, or folk tale, creating a form of extremely short short stories that incorporates poetry. On the other hand, the Qing dynasty writer Wang Chuanshan sets out in a very no-nonsense way to explode the

---

1. Stephen Owen, *Readings in Chinese Literary Thought* (Cambridge: Council on East Asian Studies / Harvard University Press, 1992), pp. 360–61. We have adapted this quote to reflect pinyin transliteration.

practices of pompous scholars and presents a plan for a rigorously mimetic poetic practice.

Wang Guowei (1877–1927) was among the foremost modern poets in the *ci* form (*ci* poems are written to metrical patterns derived originally from Central Asian songs). A professor and prolific scholar, he was widely familiar with Western philosophy and aesthetics. He was for a short time (in 1923) the tutor of the last emperor of China, Henry Puyi, who at that time was a powerless monarch tolerated by the warlords and the republican government. In 1927 Wang Guowei went to the royal Summer Palace, where he walked into Kunming Lake and drowned himself, for reasons that remain controversial. Perhaps he feared that his loyalty to the dying dynasty would cause him to be executed by the Nationalists, who were marching on Beijing, or perhaps he was overwhelmed by family or financial pressures. Some interpret his death as similar to that of Sikong Tu (who was said to have killed himself to protest Emperor Li Yu's murder). These deaths are in the Chinese tradition of moral and political protest-suicides exemplified by Qu Yuan, the exiled Confucian poet who drowned himself in the Miluo River in Hunan to warn his oblivious king of the dangers to his dynasty from the nearby state of Qin.

"Poetry is a dragon," writes Zhao Zhixin. Some critics, like Wang Chuanshan, want to seize and dissect it; others want to leave it whole and mysterious. There is a Chinese folktale about a young man who apprentices himself to a master to learn a skill with which to make a living. This master teaches him all the ways to butcher a dragon. After much effort and expense, the young man returns to his father and proudly tells him of his new skill. His father replies, "Great! But one question . . . where are you going to find a dragon?" These critics tell us where the mythical beast is laired, and though they quibble over which of many tricks and traps to use, listening in on the debates of these literary hunters suggests one essential fact: there are many ways to capture a dragon.

STORIES AND APHORISMS ABOUT LITERATURE

DURING the reign of King Renzong, some high-ranking officials famous for their poetry admired Bai Juyi's simple style, so their lines often came very easily.[2] One of them wrote such a couplet that goes:

> I have a salary to make my wife and children fat,
> but nothing goes to my yeomen and my people.

Someone teased the author: "Yesterday on the great highway I saw a carriage carrying an extremely heavy load. The oxen were straining hard against the burden. This must have been your fat wife and children!" Those who heard spread this story around as a funny joke.

from MR. SIX-ONE'S COMMENTS ON POETRY,
by Ouyang Xiu (1007–1072)

THE poets Meng Jiao and Jia Dao were both impoverished

---

2. Bai Juyi's poems often are written in a deliberately plain style, sometimes in imitation of the folk songs collected by the Music Bureau in the second century BCE. According to a popular account, Bai used to read his poems to an old peasant woman and change any line that she couldn't understand.

until their deaths, and they liked to write lines reflecting their hard lives. Meng has a poem on moving house:

> I borrow a wagon to carry my furniture,
> but my goods don't even make one load.

He is saying that he's so poor he hasn't anything to move. He has another poem to express his gratitude to people who have given him some charcoal:

> The heat makes my crooked body straight.

People say one cannot write lines like this without actually experiencing such suffering. Jia Dao writes,

> I have white silk in my sideburns
> but cannot use it to weave a warm shirt.

Even if one could weave hair, it wouldn't do him much good. Jia Dao also has a poem "Morning Hunger" with these lines:

> I sit and hear the zither on the western bed:
> two or three strings snapping in the cold.

People say that this poem shows that hunger, like the cold, is unbearable.

from MR. SIX-ONE'S COMMENTS ON POETRY,
by Ouyang Xiu (1007–1072)

MEI YAOCHEN told me that though a poet can coin his own expressions, it is very difficult to do. Only when the idea is original and the language fine and when the poem reaches a place people have never been before can this be achieved. To describe a challenging subject, you must make it visible to your reader. The poem should resonate within you after you put it down, and one should find meaning in it beyond what words express. Jia Dao writes, for example,

> I collect mountain fruit with a bamboo basket
> and fetch spring water with an earthenware pot.

This description of a remote mountain region implies that the official writing the poem has little to do. But these lines are not as good as the following ones, which say something similar:

> This country is so old the roots of the scholar tree
>   are exposed.
> The official here is so honest his horse's bones bulge
>   from its skin.

These two lines are good because they visualize a difficult subject and have a strong resonance.

Mei Yaochen says that what the author has in his heart the reader will also experience. For example:

> Moon and a thatched-roof inn. Roosters crow.
> Footprints on a frosted stone bridge.
>
> — *Wen Tingjun*

> Strange birds scream in vast fields.
> The setting sun unnerves the traveler.
>
> —*Jia Dao*

These two examples go beyond what the words describe to suggest a traveler's hardship and nostalgia.

from MR. SIX-ONE'S COMMENTS ON POETRY,
by Ouyang Xiu (1007–1072)

MEI YAOCHEN often says that though lines may be smooth, they're flawed if they are too easy and vulgar. For example, there's a couplet dedicated to a fisherman that goes:

> He doesn't see what's happening in the marketplace.
> He only hears the sound of wind and water.

Someone commented, "These are symptoms of liver and kidney disease."[3] Another person wrote this couplet about poetry:

> I look for it all day in vain.
> It comes to me at last by itself.

Originally this referred to the difficulty of finding good lines, but a jokester commented that it was a description of a lost cat, and everyone had a good laugh.

from MR. SIX-ONE'S COMMENTS ON POETRY,
by Ouyang Xiu (1007–1072)

LI CHEN was traveling as an itinerant monk, and one day, on his way to see a waterfall, he met Zen master Huang Nie, who became his traveling companion. Huang Nie said, "I have a couplet for this waterfall, but I cannot finish

---

3. The fisherman here is held up as a kind of "natural man," equivalent to the woodcutter Thoreau encounters at Walden Pond. He is so attuned to nature that even when surrounded by commerce and city life, he hears only water and wind. Ouyang is making fun of these lines by ignoring the larger context of the poem in the Chinese tradition, misreading it on purpose.

the poem." Li Chen responded, "I will complete it for you." So Huang recited:

> It travels through a thousand rocks, ten thousand
> valleys, but doesn't give up.
> Only when seen from afar do you know it comes from
> a high place.

Li Chen continued:

> How can streams and brooks restrain it?
> It finally returns to the ocean and becomes waves.

Later, Li Chen became king. This poem illustrates his ambition.[4]

from GEN XI'S COMMENTS ON POETRY,
compiled between 1174 *and* 1189 *by Chen Yanxiao*

DURING the Kaiyuan period in the Tang dynasty, Emperor Ming ordered his palace concubines to sew padded silk jackets for soldiers fighting at the border. One of the soldiers discovered a poem in his jacket, which read:

> Far traveler fighting on a sand battlefield,
> wracked with cold, how do you sleep?

---

4. Li Chen (684–762) became the Tang dynasty emperor Xuangzong. At the time of this story, Li was disguised as a monk for protection against Emperor Wuzong, who recognized him as a possible contender for the throne. Li Chen interprets the first couplet as referring both to the waterfall and to himself (both are unstoppable, both are secretly from a high place) and writes his couplet to suggest his own illustrious destiny.

My hands sewed this battle coat;
in whose hands will it fall?
I double-stitched it with passion,
I stuffed it with cotton and love.
But my life is over.
May we marry in the next.

The soldier presented the poem to the marshal, who reported the matter to the emperor. The emperor sent word through the palace for the author to step forward, without fear of punishment. One of the concubines confessed, saying, "I deserve to be killed ten thousand times." Emperor Ming was deeply moved and decreed that she should have her soldier, saying, "I'll give you your chance in *this* life."

from POETRY STORIES, *by Meng Qi (Song dynasty)*

A MAN named Xu Deyan married Princess Chen Lechang. When the country of Chen was on the verge of being conquered, the man told his wife, "When the country falls, you will certainly be taken into a powerful man's house. If your love for me doesn't die, I hope we will have the chance to be together again." So the lovers broke a mirror into two halves and promised to sell their mirror halves at the capital's market on the 15th of January in an attempt to meet again. Eventually, Chen was overrun and Princess Lechang was taken to be the woman of Yang Su, a duke from the country of Yue. Xu wrote a poem:

The mirror and the person are gone.
The mirror returns. The person doesn't.

I don't see the Moon Lady's shadow.
Bright and empty moonlight lingers.

The princess received this poem and wept without end. When Yang Su learned of this, he sent for Xu Deyan in order to return his wife. But he ordered Princess Lechang to write a poem about the situation. Her poem read:

I feel so frantic today.
New husband faces old
and I don't dare laugh or cry.
How hard it is to be a woman.

from POETRY STORIES, *by Meng Qi (Song dynasty)*

THE Tang poet Gu Kuan was touring the royal grounds in Luoyang when he found a wide leaf floating on the stream leaving the palace. On the leaf he saw a poem inscribed:

After they took me deep into the palace,
year after year I saw no spring.
Now I write a poem on this leaf
and sent it to a man who loves.

The next day Gu Kuan wrote this poem in response and released it in the water upstream from the palace:

Deep in the palace, flowers fall and nightingales are
    sad;
in Shangyan Palace a concubine bursts inside with
    grief.
The Forbidden City can't forbid water to flow east.
To whom should I address this leaf poem?

About ten days later, another visitor searched the royal grounds until he found another poem on a leaf, which he showed to Gu Kuan:

> My leaf poem escaped the Forbidden City.
> Who are you who responds with such love?
> I sigh and envy the leaf in the waves
> that drifts effortlessly into spring.

from POETRY STORIES, *by Meng Qi (Song dynasty)*

PRINCE NING was infatuated with his courtesans, and he had dozens of them, pretty and talented. To the left of his residence there lived the wife of a cakemaker, who was slender, pale, and very beautiful. The moment the prince saw her, he couldn't take his eyes off her, so he gave a huge amount of money to the husband and forced her to leave him. The prince favored her more than anyone else. After one year had passed, he asked the woman, "Do you still miss your cakemaker?" The woman was silent and didn't answer. So he summoned the cakemaker and let them meet. The wife looked at her old husband with tears in her eyes, and it seemed to be too much for her to bear. There were more than ten guests present in the prince's house, all of them famous writers and scholars, and they looked very sad on witnessing this scene. The prince ordered them to write poems about what had transpired. The senior counselor, the poet Wang Wei, was the first to finish his poem:

> Even in her favor and extraordinary
> place of today,

she can't forget her former husband.
We look at her, a flower.
Her eyes flood.
She has nothing to say to the king of Chu.[5]

from POETRY STORIES, *by Meng Qi (Song dynasty)*

GENERAL ZHU TAO didn't make a distinction between the common people and scholars when he conscripted men into his army. He asked everybody to come to the ball field,[6] then went to inspect them. There was one man who looked particularly well mannered, with an elegant stride. The general asked him, "What is your occupation?" He answered, "Writing poetry." "Are you married?" the general inquired. The scholar answered, "Yes, I am," and so the general ordered him to compose a poem to his wife on the spot. Without hesitation, the poet wrote out this poem with brush and ink:

> It's easy to brush out a poem
> but hard to carry a spear and fight.

---

5. "King of Chu" alludes to a similar case in history. In the Spring and Autumn period (770–476 BCE), the king of Chu conquered the marquis of Xi and took his wife in marriage. Although Lady Xi became the mother of two of his sons, heirs to the throne, she never spoke a word to the king of Chu. This translation was first published in Tony Barnstone, Willis Barnstone, and Xu Haixin, trans., *Laughing Lost in the Mountains: Poems of Wang Wei* (Hanover, N.H., & London: University Press of New England, 1991).

6. The field was used for the ancient team sport of *qiu*, which was somewhat like a combination of soccer and hackeysack. The soft ball was kept aloft with the feet, knees, and chest.

I'm used to snuggling with you in a warm quilt like
    mandarin ducks
and am nervous about frontier cold at the Gate of
    Cranes,
where my coat will flap loosely about an emaciated
    body
and tears will soak the pillowcase.
I will try to save my ink stick
to paint your eyebrows when I return.

Then the general asked him to write another poem in the
voice of his wife:

My long hair and hairpin are both rare things,
and I still wear my wedding gown.
It's the season to plant the crops, but nobody's here
    to work.
My man is supposed to be home by now, but no one
    comes.

The general was so impressed that he gave him some rolls
of cloth and decided not to conscript him.

from POETRY STORIES, *by Meng Qi (Song dynasty)*

CUI FU, from Boling, was very handsome, proud, and
aloof, but he failed his civil service examination. On the
Day of Pure Brightness, when people sweep off the tombs,
he visited the southern part of the capital alone. He came
to a great estate, which sprawled over an entire acre, with
blooming flowers and emerald trees. Nobody seemed to be
about, though Cui knocked at the door for a long time.

Then a girl looked through the crack between the double doors and asked him, "Who are you?" He told her his name and said, "I'm just having a spring outing alone, and I'm very thirsty." The young woman went to fetch a cup of water and opened the door, letting him into the courtyard. She drew out a bench and asked him to sit. She stood against an angled peach branch and looked at him with affection, and began to make herself attractive through subtle looks and gestures. But when Cui started flirting with her, she just gazed at him without answering. When Cui said good-bye, she walked him to the door and turned as if trying hard to hold back her emotions. Cui also kept looking back. But he didn't return to that estate for a long time. On the next Pure Brightness Day, Cui remembered that young woman. He couldn't help himself but went straight to the estate to look for her. The walls and the door looked the same, though the door was locked from the outside. So he left a poem on the left door panel:

> On this day last year, beyond this door,
> her face and peach flowers heightened each other's red.
> Where is her face now?
> Peach flowers are laughing with spring wind.

Several days later, he was on the south side of the city by chance, so he went to the house again and heard someone crying inside. Cui knocked at the door. An old man came out and asked, "Are you Cui Fu?" He answered, "Yes." The old man started to sob again, saying, "You killed my daughter!" Cui was so surprised that he didn't know what to say. The old man said, "My daughter was of age and she knew how to read, but she was not engaged. Ever since last year, I had noticed that she often wore a dazed expression. It was as if she had lost something. A few days ago, we went out. When we came back she read the characters on the left door panel, and as soon as she went into the house, she fell deathly ill. She refused to eat for days, and now she is dead. I'm an old man, and the reason my daughter was not married was that I was looking for a gentleman who would take care of me. Now she is dead, and it was you who killed her." And he broke down in tears again. Cui was also moved and asked the old man to let him in the house to weep before the body. She looked just the same, laid out on the bed. Cui cradled her in his arms and cried, saying, "I am here, I am here." After he had held her for some time, her eyelids lifted, and within twelve hours she had come fully to life again. The father was overwhelmed with joy, and he gave his blessing to the young couple's marriage.

from POETRY STORIES, *by Meng Qi (Song dynasty)*

ONE day, Zhu Qingyu met Zhang Ji, the senior secretary to the Water Board, a man with a great appreciation for Zhu's poems. Zhang asked Zhu to give him all his poems and selected twenty-six of them to carry in his long sleeves, so that he always would be able to recommend them to others. As Zhang Ji had a weighty reputation, people began to copy and recite Zhu's poems. Later, Zhu passed the civil service examination. [Shortly before the examination] Zhu wrote Zhang a poem titled "The New Bride":

Last night the red candles died out in the bridal suite.
She is waiting for dawn to greet her new family.
After making herself up she asks him softly,
"Is this way of painting my eyebrows fashionable?"

Zhang Ji answered him with the following poem:

The beauty from Yue's new makeup leaps from the
  mirror's heart.
You act reserved because you know you're gorgeous.
The rich grandes dames don't look as elegant as you.
A water-chestnut girl's song is worth ten thousand
  gold coins.

After this exchange, Zhu became famous across the land.

from THE COMPLETE TANG DYNASTY COMMENTS
ON POETRY, *vol. 3, by You Mao (1127–1194)*

JIA DAO's line "A monk is knocking at a door by moonlight" is only guess and imagination, like talking about
someone else's dream. Even if the description is extremely
accurate, it is not at all related to the heart. Those who
comprehend this point will see that this line is mere fiction,
since the poet famously cannot decide between the words
"push" and "knock." If there is a direct line from the scene
to the heart, there is no choice between "to push" and "to
knock." Only one is accurate. Emotions based on actual
scenes are spontaneous and wonderful, so why bother to de-
bate such things? For example, Wang Wei's line "Long
river. The setting sun is round" does not present a pre-
planned scene; and his line "I call to a woodcutter across

the water" is not from the imagination. Rather, they are
what the Zen masters term "immediacy."

from GINGER STUDY COMMENTS ON POETRY,
by Wang Chuanshan (also known as
Wang Fuzhi, 1619–1692)

CONSIDER these lines:

> Setting sun on the great banners.
> In the braying wind, horses neigh.

—*Du Fu*

How can one say the source of this couplet is

> The horses neigh and bray.
> The banners slowly swell.

from THE BOOK OF SONGS

With their different intentions, these sad and happy scenes
cannot borrow from each other. This is only a coincidence
of words. The problem with Song dynasty people is that
they always are looking for the source of everything. Espe-
cially those who are sour nincompoops demand a source for
every line, as if poetry were always the source of poetry. In
this way they seek self-justification and a basis for their
judgments.

Du Fu's couplet goes:

> I'm going to buy a gallon of wine
> since I happen to have three hundred bronze coins.

On this basis, they figured out the price of wine in the Tang dynasty. But Cui Guopu's lines state,

> To buy one gallon of wine
> only costs ten thousand bronze coins.

So if you buy wine from Du Fu's vendor and sell it to Cui Guopu, you can make a profit of more than thirty times your investment! Those who go looking for sources produce imbecilities such as this.

from GINGER STUDY COMMENTS ON POETRY,
by Wang Chuanshan (also known as
Wang Fuzhi, 1619–1692)

FANGSI hated the disordered fashion of writing in his time [Qing dynasty]. He commented, "Poetry is a dragon: head, tail, claws, horns, scales, and whiskers. If one is absent, it's not a dragon." The prefect scoffed, "But poetry is a magic dragon: when you see its head, you don't see its tail. Or, wreathed in clouds, it might reveal a claw or a scale. So how can you see the whole body? That's only for sculpture or for paintings." And I say: A magic dragon might coil or stretch out, and it changes without fixed shape. Although you perceive it vaguely—just one scale or one claw—you know its head and tail are there. But if you restrict yourself to what you see and take that as the whole dragon, then the painters and sculptors will have only scornful words to say to you.

from THE RECORD OF TALKS ABOUT DRAGONS,
by Zhao Zhixin (1662–1744)

Q: "What's the difference between poetry and prose?"

A: "Though the form and diction differ, the writer's message remains the same. The message is like rice. When you write in prose, you cook the rice. When you write poetry, you turn rice into rice wine. Cooking rice doesn't change its shape, but making it into rice wine changes both its quality and shape. Cooked rice makes one full, so one can live out one's life span—that's the normal course of human affairs. Wine, on the other hand, makes one drunk—makes the sad happy and the happy sad. Its effect is sublimely beyond explanation. The ideas in the Kaifeng and Xiaobian poems from the *Book of Songs* couldn't be expressed in a direct way in prose. Doesn't this show that poetry is also helpful?"

from ANSWERING WANG JILING'S QUESTIONS ON POETRY,
by Wu Qiao (Qing dynasty)

THERE is deep perception with *me* in it, and there is deep perception *without me*.[7] Consider these lines:

> With teary eyes I talk to a flower, but the flower
> doesn't respond.

---

7. The expression we translate as "deep perception" is *jing jie*, a term very difficult to nail down even in Chinese; scholars have written countless essays and at least one book debating the issue. In fact, the burden of Wang Guowei's collection of comments on poetry (the source of this commentary) is to illustrate this poetic ideal through many examples. Wang writes that "*jing* does not refer only to scenes or objects. Joy, anger, sadness, happiness are all *jing jie* in the human heart. So if you can write about real scenes, objects, emotions, you will have *jing jie*. Otherwise, not."

A chaos of red petals flies over the swing set.

> —"*To the Tune of 'Magpie on the Branch,'* "
> *by Feng Yansi*

Alone in the inn I shut the door against the cold
   spring.
The slant sun ages in the song of cuckoos.

> —"*To the Tune of 'Walking on Nut Grass,'* "
> *by Qin Guan*

These are examples of deep perception with the self in them. Now consider these:

> Gathering chrysanthemum by the east fence
> my lazy eyes meet South Mountain.

> —"*Drinking Wine," by Tao Yuanming*

> Cold waves appear, appear. A white bird hovers
> down, down.

> —"*Saying Farewell at Ying Pagoda," by Yuan Zhen*

These are examples of deep perception without the self. Deep perception with self uses the self to observe objects, so all things are colored with *me*. In deep perception without the self, objects observe objects, and one cannot tell what is *me* and what is the object.

> *from* HUMAN WORLD COMMENTS ON POETRY,
> *by Wang Guowei (1877–1927)*

In the red apricot branches spring is noisy.

The word "noisy" creates this deep perception.

> Clouds break open. Moon. The flowers play with
> shadows.

The word "play" creates this deep perception.

from HUMAN WORLD COMMENTS ON POETRY,
by Wang Guowei (1877–1927)

ONCE I was a prostitute
but now am the wife of a womanizer.
He travels and rarely comes home.
So hard to stay here in my empty bed.

—*"The Nineteen Ancient Poems," no. 2*

Why not whip your horse
ahead of others at the ferry landing?
Poverty and humility are useless,
and frustrated journeys are too much trouble.

—*"The Nineteen Ancient Poems," no. 4*

These are extreme examples of obscenity and vulgarity, but they are not taken as smutty or low poems because they are so true to life. The great *ci* poem masters in the Five Dynasties and the Northern song dynasty wrote in the same way. It's not that they didn't write obscene lines, but you don't feel them to be lewd because they sound so intimate and touching. These poets are not without vulgar vocabulary, but this just heightens the energy of their poems. The problem with obscene or vulgar language isn't the question of obscenity or vulgarity itself but rather that it may infect the poem with floating, extraneous words.

from HUMAN WORLD COMMENTS ON POETRY,
by Wang Guowei (1877–1927)

Bibliography

Ch'en, Shih-hsiang, trans. "Essay on Literature." In *Anthology of Chinese Literature, from Earliest Times to the Fourteenth Century*, edited by Cyril Birch. New York: Grove Press, 1965.

Fang, Achilles, trans. "Rhymeprose on Literature: The *Wen-fu* of Lu Chi." In *Studies in Chinese Literature*, edited by John L. Bishop. Cambridge: Harvard University Press, 1965.

Giles, Herbert Allen. *A History of Chinese Literature, with a Supplement on the Modern Period by Liu Wu-chi*. New York: Ungar Publishing Co., 1967.

Hamill, Sam, trans. *Wen Fu: The Art of Writing*. Portland, Oreg.: Breitenbush Books, 1987.

Hughes, E. R. *Lu Chi's "Wen Fu," A.D. 302: A Translation and Comparative Study*. New York: Pantheon, 1951.

Owen, Stephen, ed. and trans. *Readings in Chinese Literary Thought*. Cambridge: Harvard University Press, 1992.

Rickett, Adele. *Chinese Approaches to Literature from Confucius to Liang Ch'i-ch'ao*. Princeton: Princeton University Press, 1978.

Wang, Kuo-wei. *Poetic Remarks in the Human World: Jen Chien Tz'u Hua*. Ching-i Tu, trans. Taipei: Chung-Hwa Book Co., 1970.

———. *Wang Kuo-wei's* Jen-chien tz'u-hua, *A Study in Chinese Literary Criticism*. Adele Austin Rickett, trans. Hong Kong: Hong Kong University Press, 1977.

Wong, Siu-kit. *Early Chinese Literary Criticism*. Hong Kong: Joint Publishing Company, 1983.

Wong, W. L. "Selections of Lines in Chinese Poetry-Talk Criticism: With a Comparison between Selected Couplets and Matthew

Arnold's 'Touchstones.' " In *China and the West: Comparative Literature Studies*, edited by William Tay, Ying-hsiung Chou, and Heh-hsiang Yuan. Hong Kong: Chinese University Press, 1980.

Wong, Yoon Wah. *Ssu-k'ung T'u: A Poet-Critic of the T'ang*. Hong Kong: Chinese University of Hong Kong Press, 1976.

Yang, Xianyi, and Gladys Yang. *Poetry and Prose of the Tang and Song*. Beijing: Panda Books, 1984.

Yu, Pauline. "Ssu-k'ung T'u's *Shih-p'in:* Poetic Theory in Poetic Form." In *Studies in Chinese Poetry and Poetics*, vol. 1, edited by Ronald C. Miao. San Francisco: Chinese Materials Center, 1978.